CU00829765

The Legend Of The Holy Thorn, And Other Poems

Caruthers, Mazie V. [from old catalog]

Nabu Public Domain Reprints:

You are holding a reproduction of an original work published before 1923 that is in the public domain in the United States of America, and possibly other countries. You may freely copy and distribute this work as no entity (individual or corporate) has a copyright on the body of the work. This book may contain prior copyright references, and library stamps (as most of these works were scanned from library copies). These have been scanned and retained as part of the historical artifact.

This book may have occasional imperfections such as missing or blurred pages, poor pictures, errant marks, etc. that were either part of the original artifact, or were introduced by the scanning process. We believe this work is culturally important, and despite the imperfections, have elected to bring it back into print as part of our continuing commitment to the preservation of printed works worldwide. We appreciate your understanding of the imperfections in the preservation process, and hope you enjoy this valuable book.

The Legend of the Holy Thorn

and other Poems

BY

MAZIE V. CARUTHERS

PRINTED AT THE
SIGN OF THE

PS3505
.A7965 L4
1912

Copyrighted, 1912

MAZIE V. CARUTHERS

M ········· C
DEDICATED
TO
PETER
L·········T

Welcome none the rude folk gave
  (Oh, the Day so dreary.)
Blind their eyes, which could not see
That an holy man was he,
  Homeless, faint and weary.

So the good Saint thrust his staff
  Deep into the sod ——
Crossed it thrice in blessing there
Bade it bud and blossom fair
  To the praise of God.

Thus, a miracle he wrought,
  Centuries ago,
And since then on Christmas Morn,
Every year the Holy Thorn
  Blossoms in the snow.

THE road runs wide to Folly's Inn,
  Through pleasant fields and fair,
And scores of travelers come that way
To linger for a year or day—
  Assured of welcome there.

Here precious things—love, honor, faith
  Are lost or diced away;
Here, revel wearied, eyelids steep
And close in passion's poppied sleep,
  Till comes the reckoning day!

Then we who've lodged at Folly's Inn
  Would hide or steal away.
In vain! The Porter waits for toll.
His score each cowering, naked soul
  Must pay. God! how I pay!

THE MASKER

DAILY, I don my cap and bells
For all the world to see,
And play the role, which crucifies
The very heart of me.

But, if unshrinking, through the day
I do my bitter task,
Have I not earned the right, at night
To lay aside my mask?

THE ROAD TO YESTERDAY

THE world is fair, blue skies o'er head—
My primrose path shows gay,
And yet—betimes, I look behind
And long with all my heart to find
    The road to Yesterday.

Grass grown and faint the path may be;
No signs to point the way
Except a kiss, a memory,
A sigh, a sprig of rosmary—
    These lead to Yesterday!

What worth To-morrow's unborn hopes,
The fragrance of To-day,
When once my heart's desire and need
Is for the dim, sweet paths, that lead
    Me into Yesterday?

Came to my hearth-fire one named Sorrow.
Oh, that bleak morn, with its somber to-morrow!
From the gray skies no hope could I borrow,
Never less welcome a house-mate, than Sorrow!

Weary and long the days that we went.
Sorrow, at length, gave place to Content,
Since then, the calm of the years we have spent!
Sorrow and Joy gone—lingers Content.

BROCELIANDE

THE borders of the ancient wood
  Shut out a far world's din.
Like watchful sentinels, the trees
Whisper the pass word to the breeze,
  That we may enter in.

Within the deep heart of the wood
  Filter the pale sun beams,
Velvet with moss, grown high with fern,
The green aisle winds with many a turn—
  The very way of Dreams.

Broods silence o'er that haunted wood,
  But, on the waving grass
A shadow falls—to fade again.
'Tis Merlin and his Vivien
  Who watch us as we pass.

THE AFTERMATH

AS when the sunset's ruddy gold
Grows dull, and, gathering fold on fold
Fades quite away,—
Till but a glimmering light is seen,
The palest wraith, of what has been
A glorious day;—

In sad content, my heart and I
Resign us to our destiny—
'Tis happier so!
Let life's grey twilight shaddows fall,
If tender memories crown all
With afterglow!

'TWAS not the shame that rankled worst
       When rumor's tongue proved true—
That, I had borne courageously
       As loyal women do—

What bowed me in the dust, to wring
       Each day my heart anew,
Is knowing there has never been
       The man I thought was You—

GOD'S ACRE

WARM spring-time rain, fall softly here,
 These graves are hallowed ground—
But shower most tenderly I pray,
 Upon one little mound.

Sweet summer roses, shed your wealth
 Unstinted over all,
But where a human bud lies dead
 Let whitest petals fall.

Chill autumn winds, blow never wild
 Within this place of rest,
But croon for him a lullabye
 Of dreams on mother's breast.

Pure winter snow, float gently down
 On all the sleepers calm,
But fold my baby warm and close
 As would his mother's arm.

A MARCH DAY

A DULL grey sky,—all desolate
The fields, which seem to lie and wait
Some re-creating breath;
The bare-boughed trees make moan and sigh,
But sleeping nature lists the cry,
"Awake, from winter's death!"

A sudden, subtle change—a note
Trills sweetly from a bird's brave throat,
Of timid, patient cheer;
And earth responsive, feels the throes
Of new-born life—awakes—and knows
That spring, at last, is here.

BLIND

THE world had been peopled with shadows
    A long and dreary time,
Where I groped alone in the growing dusk,
    Till your dear hand grasped mine.

And God gave me this respite;
    One brief, sweet hour of grace,
That I might see and memorize
    The lineaments of your face!

Then, darkness fell. What matter?
    My world was n'er so bright—
For your tender eyes are my light by day,
    Your heart my rest at night!

You should be banker of all this wealth—
On condition, that once in a while
You would honor my check for an "I Love you",
And a kiss, maybe, or a smile!

A LENTEN COMPROMISE

SO, lady of most mundane ways—
Erstwhile,—turned saint for forty days,
With mien austere!
Religious-like your heart is bent
On making me give up for Lent,
Some pleasure dear?

Amen. Thus I'll make strenuous trial
To do my best at self denial,
Since you petition,
And forty days, I will eschew
My greatest joy, the sight of you,
On this condition;

If I deny myself of you,
Don't think the same return is due
In compliment!
Nay, here's my point, if you'll agree
To give up every one, but me—
I'll aye keep Lent!

VALENTINE A LA MODE

OH, dear disdainful lady mine
I want you for my Valentine.
Behold here all my stock in trade;
Much filthy lucre (Father made)
One limousine, one touring car,
A horse, at your disposal are,
A house in town—and, every May
We'll travel anywhere you say.
No crown or title do I bring,
But—money buys most anything,
And all that any mortal man
Could give you, that I swear I can!

And, counting up the final score,
Remains one trifling item more;
(Though sadly out of date, I know)
One faithful heart I give also.

"I love you"—in handwriting bold,
    But whether Jack's or Ned's,
For life of me I cannot tell—
    Both were such young hot-heads!

"My Darling's"—two or three, blaze out!
    "Devotedly your Jim"—
Dear me! How very much in love
    I thought I was with him!

"I cannot live without you, Sweet!"—
    Now, who on earth wrote this?
"I kiss your hands"—doubtless, because
    'Twas all I let him kiss!

"My own!" Oh, love's monoply
    Is bold! "My heart you broke"—
"Dearest"—My lovers' sighs, like wraiths,
    Have all gone up in smoke!

WIRELESS MESSAGES

TALK about wireless messages!
They simply are not in it
With those that lovers, far and near,
Are sending every minute.

A message never fails to reach
The heart for which 'tis meant—
"I love you" breathed into the air
Finds haven where 'tis sent.

Two hearts that beat as one know well
The code and its vibrations,
Nor miles of space can interfere
When Cupid sets up "stations"!

THE LOVERS' ALMANAC

THE almanac in which I peer
For fair or rainy weather.
Is Nancy's eyes, so darkly clear :
Sometimes, with sudden wrath they glow,
Storm signals flash, which plainly show
That clouds are going to gather ;—

Then,—when the storm has spent its force,
And tears still rain with sorrow,—
There's nothing to be done, of course,
Except to try a cautious kiss,
Which often lifts the heaviest mist,
And brings a fairer morrow!

The mercury begins to rise,
The sun shines through the rain--
All glorious now, my Nancy's eyes!
And clearing atmosphere prevails,
No storm the perfect calm assails,
My world is fair again!

TIME was, as Christmas Eve grew near,
Of Santa and his twelve reindeer,
A little lad, I sat and dreamed —
A presence real the old Saint seemed,
And on the Night of Night, I'd hark
To hear his sleigh bells in the dark,
And watch, for fear to miss his face
When he came down the chimney place.

But now, though day dreams throng my min
No trace of Santa Claus I find.
My Christmas saint has changed. Instead
Of jolly, wrinkled visage red,
Behold a lady where she stands,
The fairest maid in all the lands.
Her thrall am I for weal or woe—
Sweet Saint, whose crown is mistletoe.

Add an angler's hooks and fishing rod,
Then a book or two, for an idle mood,
'Tis when at length on the grassy sod
One's favorite author seems most good;

Stock a fat lunch box, but never leave
The savor of hunger's sauce behind,
Add the spice of adventure, a love of romance,
To a heart at rest with itself and mankind.

Then up and away, far beyond the blue hills,
While the bosky woods are yet sweet with dew,
Where Nature's heart with her secrets thrills,
And the sunshine filters one's being through!

At the ebb of day pitch a leafy tent,
Let peace settle down from the sheltering sky,
And rest, in the haven of heart's content,
While the drowsy pines croon a lullabye!

AFTER THE OPERATION

BLUR of light—faint sounds that fret
My half—awakened brain,
Returning memory, and then,
The cruel power of pain.

My crippled body craves once more
In deep, drugged sleep to lie.
So nearly spent, why may not I
Be left in peace, to die?

But, piercing through the lethargy
Which would my will enthrall
(Help, Galilean Mary-Heart!)
My little children call!

A HEART TO RENT

A heart to rent! None need apply
Except a tenant who
Will guarantee to occupy
The whole apartment through!!

Four rooms there are of goodly size,
And erstwhile there have been
As many tenants lodging there
As there is space within.

Their applications flattered me.
I hated to decline,
So portioned each his nook; inside
This roomy heart of mine.

And now I find four occupants
Too many are for me.
Since peacefully they will not live—
Each craves monopoly!

That's why I advertise: "Clean, swept,
Four empty rooms for hire!"
But no one need apply who will
Not rent the flat entire!!

SANCTUARY

WHEN I have lost the baby's ring and chewed up
    Sissy's doll,
And chased the white Angora up a a tree,
And rooted in the flower beds—my comon-sense
    suggests
To lie in hiding, might be well for me!

So, scenting future punishment, I scuttle up the
    stairs
And seek a spot to hide my guilty head,
For when my Master threatens, "Spare the stick
    and spoil the dog!"
'Tis then I hustle underneath his bed!

There's a nook 'way up against the wall, acces-
    sible to me,
Which can't be reach or prodded by his cane,
And here I crouch complacently, the while with
    growing wrath
He pokes about to oust me—all in vain!

He calls me—tempts me with a bone. I will not
    budge, not I!
"Come, Pompey!" he commands with grudging
    smile
But dogs whose brains are working well, heed no
    such siren voice;
They know that rod's in pickle all the while!

But when the kindly night has drawn a curtain
    o'er my crimes,
My blessed Mistress seeks me out, instead,
Then, with a humbly wagging tail, I dare at last,
    to leave
My vantage point beneath the Master's bed!

OMAR ON SANTA CLAUS

MYSELF when young, precociously did mock
At all the other babies on our block,
Reviling tales of Santa Claus as "fakes"
Their cherished Christmas sentiments to shock!

Yea, more especially I loved to paint
Our parents masquerading as the Saint,
And when my playmates tearfully inquired:
"AINT there A Santy Claus?" I'd scoff: "There aint"!

But now, with kiddies to the count of five,
In Santa's cause with all my skill I strive;
That day my children find he's just their Dad,
I'll be the very sorriest man alive!

THE EVOLUTION OF THE GRANDMOTHER

OH, where are the Grannies of long ago,
The kind that we find in books,
Who loved to sit and knit all day
In the sheltered ingle-nooks?
They were always garbed in softest grey,
Wore their hair in soft, little curls,
And had generous pockets of peppermints
For good little boys and girls!

They read "Pilgrim's Progress" and Baxter's
      "Saint's Rest",
And oh, 'twas variety rare
To don a best cap and go out to tea,
Or play at two-hand solitaire!
This is at least what the story books say!
Now where are those Grannies of Yesterday?

All Grandmothers now refuse to grow grey,
Or old, at the years they mock.
Hair dressed la Pompadour, trim figure hooked
Into a smart princess frock!
Garbed a la chauffeuse, she runs her own car
Young as the youngest herself,
In fact, matrimony may snare her again,
For Grandma wont stay on her shelf!

Latest French novels and problem plays serve
To amuse her by day until dinner,
Then, "Bridge" until morning, and at that gay
      game
Grandmama plays the hand of a winner!
Then where ARE the Grannies of Yesterday?

"Cultivate literature on a little oat-meal."

A REMONSTRANCE

OAT -meal for daily bread! Great Scott!
    I most decidedly will not—
Indeed, I'd never dare
    Invite the lovely Muses Nine
To breakfast, luncheon and to dine
    On such abstemious fare!

Nay—some vermouth and Gordon gin
    With bitters subtly dashed therein,
I'd joyfully mix up,
    And having warmed us up a bit
Down to good square meal we'd sit,
    And eke proceed to sup;

On chicken gumbo a Creole,
    And something served en casserole,
A salad and a sweet,
    Of brandy, just a tiny snack,
To burn upon my coffee black;
    This were a menu meet!

Then, lounging in my cushioned chair
    Puffing thick clouds of smoke in air
In after-dinner quiet,
    Nary a doubt in me would lurk
But that I shall do better work
    Than on an oat-meal diet.

THE ETERNAL FEMININE

SING a song of Spinsters!
  My latch-key and my flat!
No brutal man to say to me;
  "What have you done with that
Last dollar, I donated you
  A month or so ago?"
I love my independence, still—
  When burns the fire-light low,
I feel quite lonesome and so small—
  Mabye I'll marry, after all!

Sing a song of wedded wives!
  Three meals to plan per day,
A cook, to keep and pacify,
  A husband to "obey"!
He's very dear, of course, but when
  Both day and night, he's buried
Up to his eyes, in Wall Street stocks,
  I'ts stupid to be married.
And there are moments, when I'd fain
  Become a spinster once again!!

SPRING MILLINERY

A MAIDEN drew from its big white box
Her last year's best straw bonnet,
She twisted and turned it, but oh, dear me,!
It had "has been" writ upon it!
So she vented her rage on the innocent
thing,
Poked holes in last year-old crown,
And then, to complete its destruction quite,
On its brim danced a vicious break-down!

The sorry chapeau remained where it fell,
For several days in a corner,
When the maiden, for want of something
to do
Pulled it out, like a feminine J. Horner.
She found, that because of the twists and
the dents,
The "creation", once perched on her pate,
Presented a style very chic of its own,
And now, wore a shape up-to date!

From this, will be seen that Dame Fashion
decrees
No style is too queer, or bizarre,
And 'tis comfort to know, when outlandish
you look,
Just that much more modish you are!

AN UNSUNG HERO

WHO comes here?   A mass of wounds,
Uttering groans and awe-some sounds,
Clothes naught else save rents galore—
Broken nose a-weeping gore,
Head tied up in bloody band,
Lacking fingers on each hand—
One eye closing, t'other hid
By a strangely puffed up lid,
Black and grimy, decked with scars—
Who's this battered son of Mars?

Listen to my piteous tale
And a hero's fate bewail;
He's the man who has been showing,
In a manner vastly knowing,
His young offspring, how to throw
Fire-crackers—to make them go,
How to make the cannon roar
As they did in '64;
Shooting with a pistol too,
As "we boys used to do".

His sad condition demonstrates
What is the day he celebrates.
In short, he shows us very plain,
The glorious Fourth is here again!

THE AMATEUR HOUSEKEEPER

WHAT shall I have for dinner?
Oh, what SHALL I have to-day?
Will a mutton ragout
Be sufficient for two,
Served up with an omelette souffle?

How many vegetables?
Shall it be salad or pease,
Potatoes and beans
Or parsnips and greens?
Someone advise me, please!

What shall we eat?   Each morning
I plan for the day's supplies,
But that night, to me steals
The starved specter of meals,
And—"What for TO-MORROW?" it cries.

Breakfast, luncheon and dinner!
Three times a day without fail;
I must cudgel my brains
With scrupulous pains,
How to fill up the pampered male.

Mens' love cannot thrive on poor cooking,
(At least, so their mothers agree)
Thus, I beg on my knees
Some kind housekeeper, please
Give of your experience to me!

It's a race with the wind to challenge its speed,
A rush through vast spaces of air,
Long draughts of rare ozone, a lifting of hearts,—
A flutter of wayward loose hair!

It's a skimming of thankye'mums quick as a flash.
Going higher and higher and higher,
Till just as we're reaching the top o' the world
It's a BZZZ——TT——— and a punctured tire!"

AT BED TIME

WHEN Mother goes off visiting
  I get along all right,
And do not miss her very much
  Till bedtime comes, and night.
Of course Dad does the best he can ;
  He hears me say my prayers,
Tucks me in tight, and says "Sweet
      dreams",
  Before he goes down stairs.

But Mother sits down on the bed,
  And plays the Sand Man games.
She snoozles softly in my neck,
  And whispers honey-names.
Fathers are nice, I wouldn't trade
  Mine off for any other,
But when it's sleepy-time, I want
  To cuddle up to Mother.

THE SEVEN STAGES OF A TURKEY

(A THANKSGIVING ELEGY)

BEHOLD me! My majestic mien,
My plumage golden bronze and green,
My scornful eye!
A gobbler turkey.   Ah, full soon
An axe will strike my "crack 'o doom"—
And I must die!

Then next, when I am stark and dead—
With feathers lax and drooping head,
All done with living,
'Tis now, my carcass plump will be
Plucked, trussed,—and most uncomfortably
Stuffed for Thanksgiving.

Now see me on the serving table
Flanked 'round with ev'ry vegetab!e—
In all my glory!
The children choose (?) my legs and wings,
They'd get them anyway, poor things.
(The old, old story!)

When dinner's over. though bereft
Of half my flesh, still there is left
Some good cold meat,
And with an eye towards Friday's dinner,
Cook says,—"I' slice this'ere up thinner,
It must be eat! "

A pot-pourri, not just the same—
The festive board I grace again;
The chopping knife
With here and there a seasoning dash
Of spice,—has made me into——Hash! ! !
Oh, such a life!

Next, neatly garnished, as a stew,
I make my farewell bow to you?
Not quite ; though very weak with age,
There's still one gamut more to run
Before my pilgrimage is done—
Soup's the last stage!

At length, my bones are picked and bare,
A skeleton! The winter air
Chills me clear through!
I've served you long, you can't deny,
Still there's no doubt, you're glad as I
To say ADIEU ! !

CPSIA information can be obtained at www.ICGtesting.com
Printed in the USA
BVOW09s1940290115

385597BV00019B/273/P

9 781245 820080